The Cookie Quilt

• A TRUE STORY •

Written by **Deb Schulz** Illustrated by **Mary Josephson**

I am so excited, I can't imagine falling asleep. My mind keeps wandering—from the scent of the freshly cut Grand Fir in our living room, decorated with hand made ornaments...to the twinkling lights that dress up the bushes in our front yard. Yes, this is certainly my favorite time of the year.

And tomorrow...tomorrow will be so wonderful! No, it won't be Christmas, not quite yet. Christmas is still a couple of weeks away. Tomorrow will be Mega Cookie Baking Day! Just thinking of it makes me smile as I snuggle down a little deeper under my warm blankets and cozy patchwork quilt. Finally, I fall asleep.

"Buzz"…the alarm clock! It's 6:00 am! My wait is over! Mega Cookie Baking Day has finally arrived! I creep into my sister Amy's room to wake her. As I give her a gentle shake, I whisper "It's time to start baking."

She has traveled 700 miles to be a part of this special day. Together we quietly tip toe downstairs to the kitchen. We don't want to wake everyone else up just yet.

Amy takes the eggs and butter out of the refrigerator and adds them to our baking supplies already on the kitchen table. As I make each of us a cup of hot cocoa, we pause for a moment to look at the mountain of ingredients. Towering before us we see; fifty pounds of flour, thirty pounds of sugar, nuts, peanut butter, oil, shredded coconut, lemons, oranges and bananas. Bags of chocolate, peanut butter and butterscotch chips, many spices, bottles of flavorings, food colorings, and colored sprinkles all anxiously await for their chance to be used.

"Shall we start with something spicy this morning?" I ask Amy as she sips on her cocoa.

"Snickerdoodles would be nice..." she says with a sparkle in her eye. "Snickerdoodles it is!" I reply as I preheat the oven and turn on some quiet Christmas music.

By the time our dear friend Mary arrives, we have 180 Snickerdoodles cooling on the dining room table and a double batch of Oatmeal Raisin cookies baking.

"I bought us some muffins and sweet rolls," Mary announces. "We're going to need lots of energy today!" My daughters, Jennifer and Stephanie hear Mary come in and they too join us in the kitchen. They know wherever Mary goes…fun is sure to follow. Grandma comes in next. "I need some breakfast before I start baking," she says while rubbing her eyes. We all munch on pastries while we think ahead to what cookies we want to bake.

"Now, do you remember the rules?" I ask. Together, everyone chimes in, "There's no eating cookies, no eating dough…and if we start whining, then out we go!" "Very good!" I nod with approval and a smile.

"Ding!" goes the timer. It's time to check the Oatmeal Raisins. As I put the second batch of cookies on the table, Stephanie starts our official Cookie Tally Sheet:

Snickerdoodles – 180
Oatmeal Raisin – 205

Jennifer begins mixing a batch of her favorites—Peanut Butter & Jam Thumbprints. Mary has a batch of sugar cookies ready for the oven. Amy is searching through the cookbooks looking for her special Scotcharoo recipe, while Grandma grabs the washcloth to start in on the dishes. She sure has her work cut out for her today!

By late morning we are in full swing. The music gets a little louder and we are all singing, "It's beginning to look a lot like Christmas." And it is! Batches of gingerbread and sugar cookies are waiting to be frosted.

Next to the cooling rack Mary is whipping up some icing. Stephanie is topping the Peanut Blossoms with Hershey's Kisses. After she finishes each cookie sheet, she pops a Kiss in her mouth as well.

Amy and Grandma are singing a duet by the sink "Silver bells, silver bells, it's Christmas time in the city." I start mixing some Cowboy Cookies, the kind my grandma baked for us when we were little. Just as I am adding the chocolate chips, the phone rings. It's our friends from down the block. "What's the count?" they ask. I proudly reply, "948...and going strong!" "Keep up the good work, we'll check back with you later!"

A few hours pass and the dining room table is getting quite crowded with cookies. I begin stacking the cooled cookies and arranging them in a crazy quilt fashion. "We're getting kind of hungry." I hear a voice coming from the living room—which has been designated as the official decorating area.

I know if we are going to have the energy to bake for twelve more hours, we had better get some lunch. I head off to the deli down the street and Mary keeps the oven busy with her shortbread. You have to keep the oven full on Mega Cookie Baking Day! Tummies too! After we finish our sandwiches, we all feel much better. Throughout the afternoon we mix, bake, decorate and count the cookies. We sing, dance and laugh so much that the time flies by very quickly.

Evening approaches and Jennifer turns on the Christmas lights outside. Their red, yellow, green and blue colors shine through the foggy windowpanes. Although it's quite cold outside, the busy oven keeps the inside of our house nice and toasty. Grandma plugs in the Christmas tree lights and sits back in her favorite chair to enjoy the beauty of it all. She is especially fond of the bright star shining at the top of the tree. The carefully wrapped gifts underneath the tree seem to have captured her attention as well. Which one is for her?

Just then the doorbell rings. It's my brother David and his son Stevie! They have come by to visit for a while. Now all of Grandma's children are home and she is as pleased as can be.

David and Stevie are amazed at the sight of all of the cookies. Gladly they help with the decorating. David spreads the frosting and Stevie adds the sprinkles.

"How about ordering some pizza for dinner?" Stephanie asks. "Good idea" I say, as I pick up the phone to call for three large pizzas to be delivered. Soon our dinner arrives and we are ready for the final stretch of Mega Cookie Baking Day!

By 11:00 at night, we are back into the quieter Christmas music. Humming along to the tune of Silent Night, each one of us is moving a little slower, with a little less enthusiasm. In its place is a warm feeling of accomplishment.

The mountain of ingredients on the kitchen table has now dwindled down to a few small mounds. The dining room table however, is looking mighty fine—proudly holding thousands of colorful cookies.

As the clock in the hallway strikes midnight, Amy puts away the cookbooks and Mary finishes mixing our last batch of Eggnog Cookies. Grandma puts the leftover ingredients back into the pantry, while Jennifer and Stephanie "rest their eyes."

I pull the card table up next to the dining room table, as we still have cookies baking and the table is full to overflowing already!

A little before 2:00 am…twenty hours after we started…the last cookie is baked and counted… and the last dish has been washed and put away.

"What's the final count?" Grandma wants to know. "Are you ready?" I ask trying to contain my excitement. "3,724!"

"Wow!" Mary and Amy say as they survey the table. The four of us stare at the cookies, simply amazed. We wake the girls and offer them each a cookie. All of us choose one and we take our first bites. "Mmmmm...these are scrumptious!"

Looking over the twenty-nine different batches of cookies, carefully arranged on the table, someone comments that it looks kind of like a garden of cookies. "You know," I say, "I think it looks more like a quilt. A giant cookie quilt!"

Smiles creep across everyone's faces in agreement. We have done a fine job. And tomorrow, we will begin sharing our delicious cookie quilt with our families, neighbors and friends.

It needn't be cookies, or even something to eat ... any gift made with love is always a treat!

CPSIA information can be obtained
at www.ICGtesting.com
Printed in the USA
LVIC062044050619
620278LV00001B/12